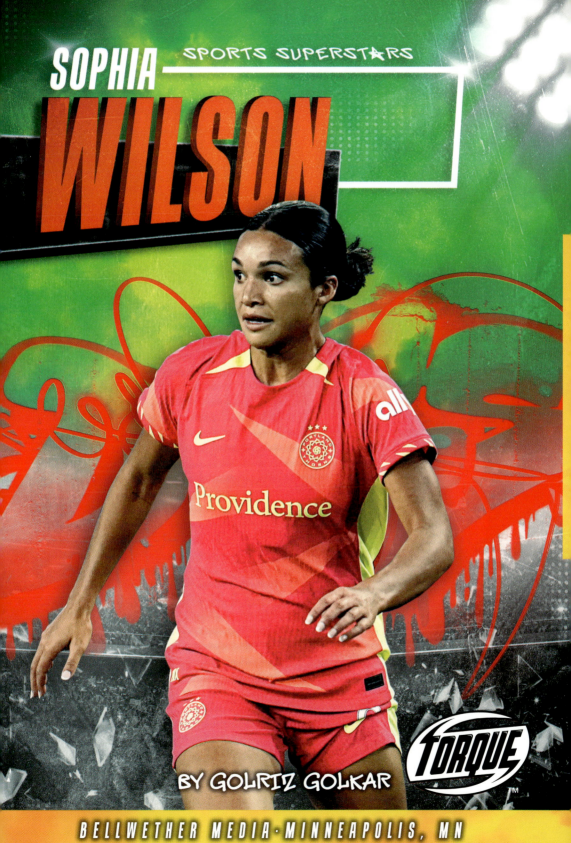

Torque brims with excitement perfect for thrill-seekers of all kinds. Discover daring survival skills, explore uncharted worlds, and marvel at mighty engines and extreme sports. In *Torque* books, anything can happen. Are you ready?

This edition first published in 2026 by Bellwether Media, Inc.

No part of this publication may be reproduced in whole or in part without written permission of the publisher. For information regarding permission, write to Bellwether Media, Inc., Attention: Permissions Department, 3500 American Blvd W, Suite 150, Bloomington, MN 55431.

Library of Congress Cataloging-in-Publication Data

LC record for Sophia Wilson available at: https://lccn.loc.gov/2025013773

Text copyright © 2026 by Bellwether Media, Inc. TORQUE and associated logos are trademarks and/or registered trademarks of Bellwether Media, Inc. Bellwether Media is a division of FlutterBee Education Group.

Editor: Kieran Downs   Designer: Gabriel Hilger

Printed in the United States of America, North Mankato, MN.

TABLE OF CONTENTS

GOAL!!!	4
WHO IS SOPHIA WILSON?	6
A YOUNG SOCCER STAR	8
SOCCER SUPERSTAR	14
WILSON'S FUTURE	20
GLOSSARY	22
TO LEARN MORE	23
INDEX	24

GOAL!!!

It is the women's soccer **semifinal** at the 2024 Paris **Summer Olympics**. The game is coming to a close. The United States and Germany are tied 0–0. Mallory Swanson chases the ball. She passes it to Sophia Wilson.

In a flash, Wilson shoots the ball into the **goal**. The U.S. wins the game! They move on to the **finals**!

WHEN I GROW UP

As a child, Wilson wanted to either play sports or host a design TV show when she grew up.

5

WHO IS SOPHIA WILSON?

Sophia Wilson is a soccer player. She plays **forward**. Wilson plays in the **National Women's Soccer League** (NWSL). She is also on the U.S. Women's National Team (USWNT).

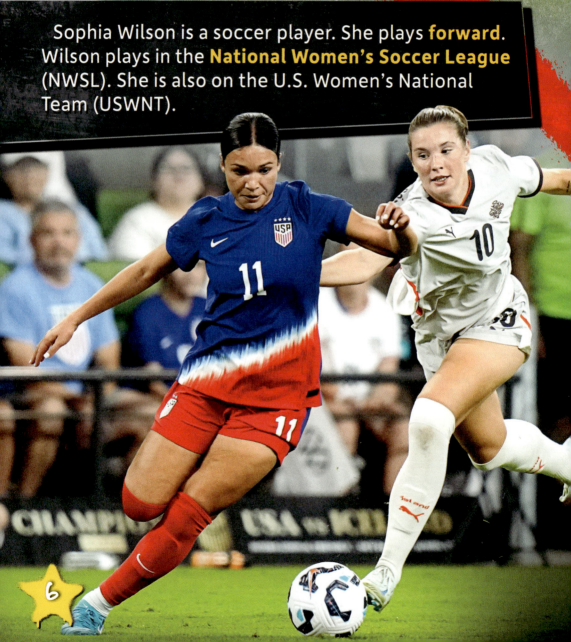

SOPHIA WILSON

BIRTHDAY	August 10, 2000
HOMETOWN	Windsor, Colorado
POSITION	forward
HEIGHT	5 feet 6 inches
DRAFTED	Portland Thorns in the 1st round (1st overall) of the 2020 NWSL Draft

Wilson became a star soccer player at a young age. Her goals have led her teams to win many **championships**.

7

A YOUNG SOCCER STAR

Wilson started playing for youth soccer clubs at age 5. In 2011, she joined Arsenal Colorado. In 2012 and 2013, she helped the team win state championships.

WILSON AND HER FATHER

ATHLETIC FAMILY

Wilson's father and two sisters all played basketball. Wilson also played basketball as a child before choosing to focus on soccer.

In 2014, she joined the Real Colorado club. Wilson played with them during her high school years. They played against other teams across the country. Wilson was a top player.

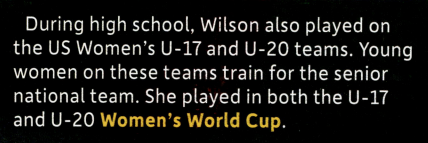

During high school, Wilson also played on the US Women's U-17 and U-20 teams. Young women on these teams train for the senior national team. She played in both the U-17 and U-20 **Women's World Cup**.

Wilson finished high school in 2018. Many colleges wanted Smith to play for their soccer teams. Wilson chose Stanford University.

U-17 WOMEN'S WORLD CUP

Wilson was a standout player at Stanford. In 2018, Wilson's many goals led the team to a winning season. But she broke her ankle. She missed many games.

12

Wilson got better and came back stronger. In 2019, she led her team to the **NCAA** Championship! Wilson finished the season with 17 goals in 21 games.

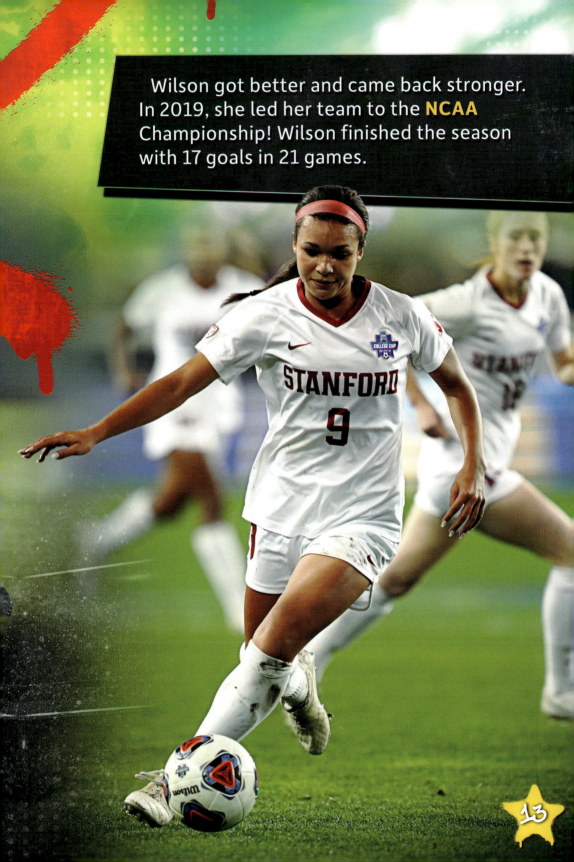

SOCCER SUPERSTAR

2020 NWSL DRAFT

Wilson decided to leave Stanford in 2020. She was the top pick in the NWSL **Draft**.

Wilson joined Portland Thorns FC. But a hurt ankle and shutdowns due to **COVID-19** slowed Wilson down. She healed and came back strong in 2021. She helped the Thorns win the **NWSL Shield**.

SOPHIA WILSON MAP

- Portland Thorns FC, Portland, Oregon — 2020 to present
- U.S. Women's National Team, Chicago, Illinois — 2020 to present

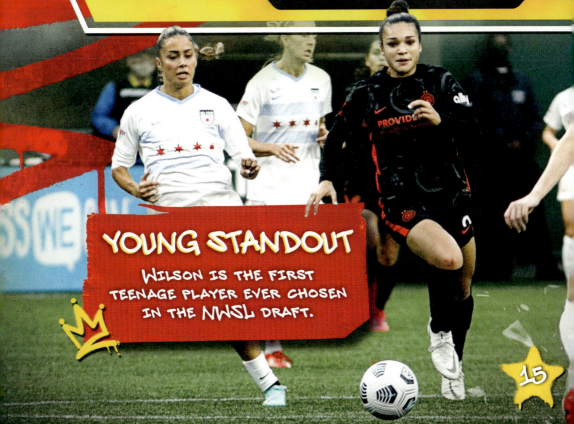

YOUNG STANDOUT
Wilson is the first teenage player ever chosen in the NWSL draft.

15

Wilson was a standout player in 2022. She scored 14 goals that season. Wilson's goals led the Portland Thorns to the NWSL Championship.

Wilson was named the NWSL Championship **Most Valuable Player** (MVP). She also became the 2022 NWSL regular season MVP. Wilson won the U.S. Soccer Female Player of the Year Award.

2022 NWSL CHAMPIONSHIP

Wilson joined the USWNT team at the 2023 Women's World Cup. Wilson played well. But her team did not win. Wilson did not give up. She and the USWNT headed to the 2024 Paris Summer Olympics.

Wilson scored three goals, including two in one game. The team won the gold medal!

2024 PARIS SUMMER OLYMPICS GOLD MEDAL

TIMELINE

— 2019 —
Wilson helps Stanford win the NCAA Championship

— 2020 —
Wilson is drafted by the Thorns

— 2022 —
Wilson and the Thorns win the NWSL Championship

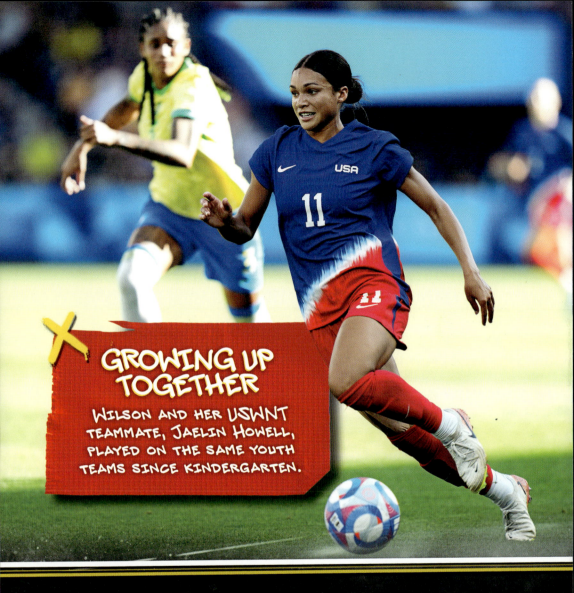

GROWING UP TOGETHER

Wilson and her USWNT teammate, Jaelin Howell, played on the same youth teams since kindergarten.

— 2023 —
Wilson plays in the Women's World Cup

— 2024 —
Wilson and the USWNT win the Olympic gold medal

WILSON'S FUTURE

Wilson works with a project called Create the Space. The project works to give **mental health** support to people who play sports. She also works with companies that sell sports products.

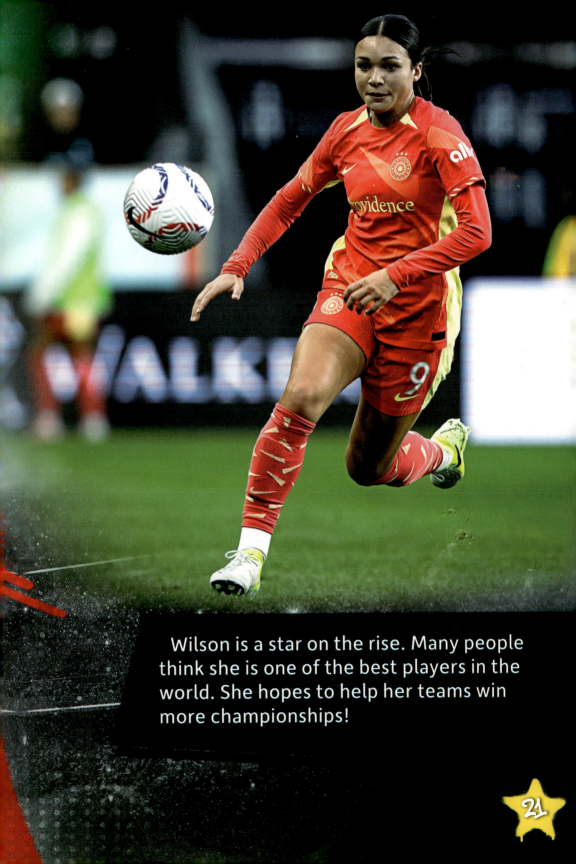

Wilson is a star on the rise. Many people think she is one of the best players in the world. She hopes to help her teams win more championships!

GLOSSARY

championships—contests to decide the best team or person

COVID-19—a virus that led to shutdowns and millions of deaths around the world

draft—a process during which professional teams choose high school and college athletes to play for them

finals—the championship series of a sports tournament

forward—a position in soccer that involves trying to score or help teammates score goals

goal—either net on a soccer field that players shoot the ball into to score a point; points in soccer are also called goals.

mental health—the way people think and feel about themselves and the world around them

most valuable player—an award given to the best player of a sport

National Women's Soccer League—a professional women's soccer league at the top of the U.S. soccer league system

NCAA—National Collegiate Athletic Association; the NCAA is in charge of student athletes at colleges in the United States.

NWSL Shield—an annual award given to the NWSL team with the most points that season

semifinal—a game played to determine which team plays in the final game of a sports tournament

Summer Olympics—a worldwide summer sports contest held in a different country every four years

Women's World Cup—an international soccer competition held every four years; the Women's World Cup is the world's largest women's soccer tournament.

TO LEARN MORE

AT THE LIBRARY

Gish, Ashley. *National Women's Soccer League.* Minneapolis, Minn.: Bellwether Media, 2025.

Hill, Anne E. *Sophia Smith vs. Abby Wambach: Who Would Win?* Minneapolis, Minn.: Lerner Publications, 2025.

Marthaler, Jon. *US Women's Professional Soccer.* North Mankato, Minn.: Abdo Publishing, 2019.

ON THE WEB

Factsurfer.com gives you a safe, fun way to find more information.

1. Go to www.factsurfer.com

2. Enter "Sophia Wilson" into the search box and click 🔍.

3. Select your book cover to see a list of related content.

INDEX

Arsenal Colorado, 8
awards, 14, 16, 17, 18
championships, 7, 8, 13, 16, 21
childhood, 5, 8, 9, 10, 19
COVID-19, 14
Create the Space, 20
draft, 14, 15
family, 8
favorites, 11
forward, 6
goal, 4, 7, 12, 13, 16, 18
hurt, 12, 14
map, 15
National Women's Soccer League, 6, 14, 16
NCAA Championship, 13
NWSL Championship, 16
NWSL Shield, 14
Portland Thorns FC, 14, 16
profile, 7
Real Colorado, 9
record, 15
Stanford University, 10, 12, 14
Summer Olympics, 4, 18
timeline, 18–19
trophy shelf, 17
U.S. Women's National Team, 4, 6, 10, 18, 19
Women's World Cup, 10, 11, 18

The images in this book are reproduced through the courtesy of: Soobum Im/ Contributor/ Getty Images, front cover; Ira L. Black - Corbis/ Contributor/ Getty Images, pp. 3, 21; John Todd/ ISI/ Contributor/ Getty Images, p. 4; Andrea Vilchez/ ISI/ Contributor/ Getty Images, p. 5; Independent Photo Agency Srl/ Alamy Stock Photo, p. 6; Steph Chambers/ Contributor/ Getty Images, p. 7; Fiona Goodall - FIFA/ Contributor/ Getty Images, p. 8; Brad Smith/ ISI Photos/ USSF/ Contributor/ Getty Images, pp. 9, 20; Boris Streubel - FIFA/ Contributor/ Getty Images, p. 10; runrun2, p. 11 (coffee); Elnur, p. 11 (reading); Susan Vineyard, p. 11 (English); Alex Grimm - FIFA/ Contributor/ Getty Images, p. 11 (Sophia Wilson); Cody Glenn/ Contributor/ Getty Images, p. 12; John Todd/ ISI Photos/ Contributor/ Getty Images, p. 13; Jose L. Argueta/ ISI Photos/ Contributor/ Getty Images, p. 14; Ray Terrill/ Wikipedia, p. 15 (Portland Thorns stadium); John Rudoff/ Sipa USA via AP/ AP Images, p. 15 (Sophia Wilson); Brad Smith/ ISI Photos/ Contributor/ Getty Images, pp. 16, 17, 18 (2024 Paris Summer Olymics gold medal, 2022), 19 (Sophia Wilson); Stanford University/ Wikipedia, p. 18 (Stanford logo); Portland Thorns FC/ Wikipedia, p. 18 (Portland Thorns FC logo); 2023 FIFA Women's World Cup/ Wikipedia, p. 19 (2023); Eurasia Sport Images/ Contributor/ Getty Images, p. 19 (2024); Kim Price/ AP Images, p. 23.